The Agenda

"Wake up Black America! Now is your time!"

By

Mansa Mnēmē

© 2018 by Mansa Mnēmē M.B.
First published by Verengai Publishing House
07/16/2018

ISBN 978-0-9995371-4-5

The Agenda "Wake-up Black America! Now is your time."
Copyright © 2018,2019 by Memory Bengesa All rights reserved. Printed in the United States of America. No part of this book may be used or reproduced in any manner whatsoever without the written consent of its author.
Verengaipublishing@gmail.com

Contents

Disclaimer   4

The Agenda   5

Become   19

Own   31

React   41

Never   53

Freedom   56

Rumors   60

Embrace   64

Evolve   73

Disclaimer

First and foremost, I understand that history is not for everyone, so please bear with the first section of this book, as I have to explain **THE AGENDA** before I put it in context so that everything else, I have written would make sense to you.

In this book, I use the references "white" and "white men/women" a lot. Please understand that those terms do not describe all white people, as I'm aware that not everyone in America is racist or prejudiced, and not all super-rich white people belong to the elites.

Also note, that I only use the terms "nigger," "negro," "African" or "Black American" to represent the eras under consideration. I am one hundred percent black and I already know it does not necessarily give me an automatic pass. So, let's begin….

The Agenda

1917

East St. Louis Massacre. Woodrow Wilson was the president of this era. As soon as he was sworn into office, he had work to do! East St. Louis was brewing with local matters that would grab national attention. During the great migration of the African Americans from the south to northern states, most black Americans found themselves on a one-way trip to East St. Louis. Back in those days, communication was by word of mouth within the black community.

People of the white middle and lower class were demanding for more wages from their employers. Little did they know that their fellow countrymen did not feel like they owed them a dime. Therefore, in the urgency of white business owners to keep their businesses running, they opened their factories and warehouses to the Negroes. Because of this, there were records of as many as 2,000 Negroes traveling to East St Louis for work in a week. Before this time, the jobs were mainly occupied by white immigrants and white union workers.

The black man was desperate to work, make an earnest wage and raise his family… such an epitome of "the American Dream, right? Well, wrong! For a while the black man was struggling to make a decent living, the white middle and lower class began to feel threatened. At this time, the white union workers were on strike, and the small business owners needed to keep things afloat, with no time to feed the ego of their striking white workers. Noticing that their jobs were being taken by black Americans—the same black Americans that used to work for free as slaves, the striking white men were enraged and mobilized themselves against the blacks.

The actions of the white business owners were unjustifiable, and they were now in a fix, so instead of admitting that they betrayed their own kinsmen, they quickly pointed fingers at the Negroes. Yet these were the same Negroes who were keeping revenue flowing into the capitalist-elitist-white-businesses.

The truth was clear as day, but it was easier for the white people to take their anger and frustrations on the black community in East St Louis, a community of people that hadn't come looking for trouble, to begin with.

1921

Little Africa Massacre (Tulsa, Oklahoma). 1918 marked the end of the First World War. The surviving war heroes eventually made their way back "Home" to the good old American grounds. World War 1 was significant to the black Americans who lived in that time for a number of reasons, chief of which was that they were still treated as second-class citizens, and most blacks had expressed their disinterest in the war. They would rather America worked on her domestic issues concerning the unfair treatment of Negroes. While a majority of young and middle-aged whites fought in the war, many black southerners continued to migrate north, in search of work and better living conditions.

By 1921, Tulsa Oklahoma was a bubbling hub for the Negroes. They had established strong communities—churches, banks, schools, hospitals, restaurants, shops, movie theaters and big mansions. This was majorly as a result of the oil surge in that area and the thorough understanding of the value of the black dollar in the black community. The concept of the black dollar emerged from the vehemence with which whites disallowed Negroes from shopping, dining or lingering in their community. The young white World War 1 returnees were not happy with the robust life the black American communities had built. They had returned to the country they had fought for only to become jobless. My speculation is that most of these men were too proud to even conjecture a situation in which they would ask a Negro business owner for a job.

During this time, Oklahoma hadn't even established laws against lynching. Most men tend to be alike when it comes to matters of the heart; they all want to work and provide for their families. The America, these white soldiers of Tulsa, had left behind had changed while they were at war. There is nothing that causes a white man to feel threatened like a successful Negro. And just the thought of a Negro being financially better than a white middle, upper or lower-class man was enough catalyst for hate and retaliation.

White supremacists are all about power, control, and dominance. And whenever they feel like they are losing hold on this power, they go to dangerous lengths to "protect" it. The fear of losing their "place" is so real to them. If you're wondering how I know, just take a look at the current president in 2018. The white elite (politicians, local and national business owners, family heirs, etc.) deceptively whispered in the ears of the frustrated young white war veterans of Tulsa, Oklahoma. The lies must have gone something like; *"Why you don't have any jobs is because the Negroes took them all. Look at them! They are living in mansions and even have the audacity to build their own community."*

These group of elites were not interested in the welfare of the younger war veterans. They probably just wanted to start chaos, so they could have total control of their wealth. The only thing the elites really shared with the war veterans was the color of their skin. Sadly, skin tones can leave people feeling like they are the same, but in reality, the elites are usually only interested in wealth accumulation and power retention… and it doesn't matter who dies and what pawns they use; even their own—white people. As long as you're not in their social class, you are all fair game, regardless of whether you are White, Black, Hispanic or Asian.

Seething in anger and frustration, most young white veterans across America joined the Ku Klux Klan between 1918 and 1921. Of course, we have the movie *"Birth of a nation,"* to thank for reviving the once dying Klan by larger numbers. The pattern is that when the middle- and lower-class white man was upset, he simply took it out on everything else but himself and the deceptive lies of the elites who are actually using him for their financial benefit.

On **May the 31st in 1921**, the whites put their hateful plan into action. Fueled by rage and envy, the mobs of white men, law enforcement included, gathered outside *Little Africa* also known as *Negro Wall Street* of Tulsa Oklahoma. The law enforcement deputies were members of the Klan at that time. They had been sworn in, so the killings of Negroes would be justified by the law.

Unknown to the Black Americans of Tulsa, the war had shown up in their neighborhood while they were unprepared. Before arriving in *Little Africa*, the white men made sure that they had cut and burnt down the telephone lines and telegraph communications going in and out of the black community.

They blocked the railroad tracks to make sure that no one would escape. They had literally come to Steal, Kill and Destroy. The white men who were equipped with guns and ammunition, went from door to door, spraying bullets through the walls of the houses in *Little Africa*.

There was no mercy for the Negro mothers, children, surgeons, business owners, or servicemen; they were all fair targets. Some white mobs shot, while others burnt the houses down after the white women looted silverware, purses, jewelry and anything else of value they could lay their hands on. Some white men searched and stole money from the bodies of the Negroes whom they had just slain like hogs.

On this day, the whites of Tulsa, Oklahoma were a well-organized mob comprising of shooters, looters, and arsonists. They degraded the corpses of the Negroes and desecrated them across telephone poles, trees and anything else they could hang their bodies on. *Little Africa* was no more, just because the Negro who had once been looked down upon had finally attained a success of his own, apparently without the permission of the white man. Had these white men been wise, they would have known that they had been played by their own government. The government that sent them to war should have been responsible for them when they returned, not the Negroes of Tulsa.

Clearly, it would have been too much for the white veterans to turn on their own people. So, if there was a scapegoat, it had to be the Negroes… paying for something that didn't have anything to do with them.

1921-2016

We have all observed that a lot has happened in the black communities between 1917 and 2016; the tragedies, neglect, modern-day lynching by law enforcement, and mass incarceration of young black men, all in efforts to eradicate the black people. However, to keep the flow of this book going, we'll not go into further details as this is not a complete History book.

*(Disclaime*r: I am not a politician, nor do I have any party affiliations. I am just an observer of paths and patterns).

In November 2016, the prevailing choice for presidency in America was a man who embodies the elite or members of the ruling class. These are super rich white people who have so much influence that they can buy a president… except for this time, he is the president. Do hold that thought for a bit.

Donald Trump ran his campaign in a very clever and classical fashion. He did what the white elite have been doing for years; he took his campaign to small American towns… towns where diversity is obsolete and mining companies have ceased to exist. He promised this hardworking middle and lower class white Americans hope. His entire campaign was designed around the concept of "hope."

At this point, it is important to note that by 2016, most American jobs had already been placed beyond the borders of the country for cheap labor. The truth is that most, if not all of the American companies that outsourced their businesses had enough wealth to profitably keep the jobs in America to support American families. But the United States is a capitalist country where it is all about the money. If these companies could get more from outsourcing while spending less on labor, then why not?

During the presidential campaigns, I traveled through rural Missouri and rural Illinois. These small towns looked very pitiful and bare, with a lot of closed warehouses. I would often find myself asking the townspeople about the history of such towns. Most people said that these were coal mining and manufacturing towns when white people migrated into them for work back in the day. They would then confidently express how hopeful they were that Donald Trump would change things in their dead towns.

I, on the other hand, having lived in and traveled through many urban and metropolitan towns, saw this paradigm shift coming long before Donald Trump started campaigning. My deduction from my rural travels is that many people are still terribly misinformed and as such, mentally living in the past. These types of people represent a recipe for disaster. My sentiments are that anyone aware of the usage of coal in 2016 or even 2018 would clearly see that the paradigm shift of energy conversion doesn't go backward, but forward. Going forward also means that energy, water, and food technology are advancing wider and faster than we can say "next presidential candidate." If I was a farmer living in rural America, I would only be a little nervous about farming… you don't need a book for that, your local grocery stores can give ideas on where farming is headed. But I digress.

My point is that the white elites are the ones behind the chaos we now grapple with, all so they can keep their pockets plump. They have to find legal and humane ways to use the white middle and lower class to carry out their agenda. Of course, the elite would never get their hands dirty; exactly the reason slavery occurred in America in the first place.

All they do is whisper into the ears of people who already feel threatened by black people. In case you didn't know, let me bring you up to speed. Your ancestors' freedom was obtained through bloodshed, and the fact that some white people wanted to keep slavery going is still a problem today. Some white people, especially the paranoid ones, still think that black people are waiting for a day for revenge. All of these factors form a convenient foundation on which the elite have built their inciting lies. The white middle and lower economic class would easily buy into their manipulation, gullible enough to think the elite have their best interest at heart because they share the same skin tone.

In the real world, the upper-class white American would never break bread or converse meaningfully with anyone considered lower on the social and economic food chain. As a matter of fact, they are repulsed by such people.

THE AGENDA is total control of wealth by the elite, and the restriction of that wealth within their bloodline, as well as the continuous rule over America with the influence of their riches.

THE PATTERN is deception. In Tulsa, when the white men came back from World War 1, the evidence was clear as day; the government, made of some elite, sent them overseas to fight a war that wasn't America's, to begin with, just so they could make more money. Apparently, wars are big payouts. And when these war veterans came back to nothing, (sound familiar in recent times?) The elite had to blame it on the Negroes.

Black people were hitherto not liked by some whites, and that naturally fueled their envy and rage. When we examine the massacre in East St Louis in 1917, we see that the greedy elitist businessmen grew tired of their own people because of the union, and they knew that blacks needed to work and were willing to do so for whatever they could be paid without complaining.

When the blacks started working, minding their own business, the ruling class once again whispered in the itchy ears of their white middle and lower-class pawns. Woodrow Wilson was president of the United States at the time and was in pursuit of tax breaks for small businesses, banking system reforms, as well as import tariffs. These issues suddenly became rather pressing for him because the elite really does have a way of buying a president, especially as campaigns are expensive and must be funded by someone.

The ruling class is simply ruthless. Their play goes something like this; "What are you going to do for *me,* so *I* can become wealthier? And in return, I will see what I can do for you."

The white elite may have little consideration for lower class white people, but they certainly have none for black Americans. Blacks cannot be entitled to the generational wealth and power that oozes out of the pores of the ruling class of America. However, I really hope this will change as we evolve.

For the 2016 elections, the average white citizens were once again subjected to the deception of the elite. The slogan, like Woodrow Wilson's, stated "hope, promise and restoration" for the white middle and lower-class Americans, when in reality, it was the biggest chess play in history. The only thing the campaign and election did was to revive the same spirit of rage, envy, and hatred among a great number of white Americans. This time, the narrative and blame game had to be worse to be more impactful so why not include immigrants as well?!

The ruling class of America is very clever. As an immigrant myself, who has undergone the thorough immigration processes, I can tell you that the government knows exactly what is going on. They set up their immigration system in a way that counteracts the ability of a family to gain right standing, just so that they can throw around accusations of "undocumented" immigrants. But has anyone ever wondered how they know the exact number of people who are supposedly "undocumented?" Undocumented means "no documentation," right? So, who is counting? All of these elaborated immigration complaints appear to be part of a system of "planned chaos" and political tactics. The government is aware of the filing system for which immigrants pay thousands of dollars, yet, the issue still makes a great recipe for hate whenever it has to be addressed.

Become

    I called my father on this particular day in 2018, as I didn't know where else to turn. I was hurt, and a little scared, and I didn't like either feeling. After I talked to my father, my decision was clear. I knew that I did not want to subject another black or brown skin to this mess. Something had to change! It is disgusting that I am still dealing with the same problems that my father dealt with, yet my father is well retired in his sixties, and I am in my thirties. I felt an overwhelming sense of responsibility and courage to take control of the situation.

    In order to be the change agent, I had to take a bold step. That fateful Sunday after my vacation ended, I sent my resignation letter to the organization for which I had been working. That was my solo protest. I decided to refuse to be oppressed any further through wages. My exit plan was initially scheduled for 2020. However, it came sooner than anticipated. I simply decided that I would no longer be subjugated by another because "they" felt that I needed the paycheck. I am fully aware that my move was radical, and I am not insinuating that Black Americans arbitrarily quit their jobs. I already had financial backing and my ducks in a row, so it wasn't much to consider in terms of financial losses.

Do allow me to walk you through the background of my story. Prior to my summer vacation, scheduled for June 4th – 10th, something unprecedented happened. My boss called me on May 31st, at about 3:45pm. My team and I were returning from a trip. He called to tell me I was getting a "Final write-up." I was shocked out of my mind. I finally rallied and asked what it was for. He mentioned that it was for an event that occurred in April, with full details contained in a memorandum that had been mailed to me. I mumbled some unintelligible thing which must have been a request for the paperwork, as I assumed that when I read it, it would make some more sense to me.

I got home, and the first thing I did was to fire up the computer. I had read this MEMO before, but I had to read it again. It had been emailed to me on May 16th, and it had to do with Laboratory tests. The MEMO stated that the disciplinary actions handed to managers would begin immediately (May 16th). The Lab mistakes that I received a "Final Write-up" for were those made by three clinicians in the month of April. The company had us take LAB competency tests in April, which would allow the company to keep their laboratory certification and credentials through a major authorizing organization.

The clinicians had taken the lab quizzes, and two of them had failed, necessitating repeat testing. These tests were carried out by the clinical department, of which I wasn't a part. When the two clinicians repeated their tests, they were allegedly spoon fed with answers, as the organization needed them to pass in order to maintain its lab licensing; even if it meant certifying incompetent clinicians.

On June 1st, before I left for my vacation, the lab suddenly published the new "official" policies and disciplinary actions for those that did not abide by the new policies. I immediately sent an email to my boss and the Human Resources Manager to ask why I was handed a Final write-up, as I was certain I had no prior disciplinary actions on my record. If I did, someone would have spoken to me, and we would have signed some paperwork.

I activated the option of notification of time of receipt for my emails. That Friday, my boss responded with his usual one-word answer. Please note that I had been working for this company for close to 14 years both in management and as a clinician, and I had never had any issues. I was one of those employees who believed in excellence, often times working as though it were my personal business, just because my grandmothers trained me that way.

I had to send that reply because I understood the process of disciplinary actions, and also took my career seriously. I really wanted to know how my boss skipped steps one, two and dove into step three of the disciplinary action protocol. I wanted someone to explain to me how a squeaky-clean employee goes from nothing to "Final."

I started my vacation on the 4th of June and scheduled a doctor's appointment for the same day. The situation at work weighed me down, as I felt like I had been a good employee. I never complained, never begged off except two times that the company was well aware of, owing to my cluster headaches… And even then, I would ensure that the team was going to be fine in my absence. I mean, who makes those types of considerations? Most employees I worked with would beg off work if they so much as sneezed.

I received sound advice in which it was suggested I send an email to the CEOs and all top executives since Human Resources had not replied my e-mail. He initially encouraged me to go talk to the head of Human resources face-to-face, which would have honestly been a better move except for one thing. I lived in a different state, and the corporate offices were over nine hours' drive away, so I went the email route.

I filled out my final write-up (there is a portion for the employee to explain their side) stating that I was contesting the "Final Write-up," on the grounds that I do not have any prior disciplinary records, the enacted policies of June 1st contradicted what my boss had given me and the fact that it was unthinkable that I should get written up over work that was done by their own incompetent clinicians who were passed for competent by their own clinical department. Something certainly wasn't right!

After the mass email distribution, I finally heard from the Human Resource department. They scheduled a call for the next day, and I patiently waited for it. When the call came in, I thought we could at least resolve the matter. I wasn't even expecting them to withdraw the "Final write-up" because that would mean admitting their mistake; something they could never do.

Anyway, I got on the phone with the Vice President of Human Resources and the Manager of Human Resources, supposedly the two most important people trusted to protect employees. I introduced myself, and the manager on the other end cut in almost immediately, "I know who it is!" All my life,

I've always handled myself with class, professionalism, and dignity, so I wasn't going to be bothered by the manager's attitude. She went on to connect me to the VP of Human resources.

The Manager of Human Resources took the lead as the conference call began. She started off by stating how disappointed she was in me. She said I could have just called her directly instead of sending mails to the company executives, and she then informed me that they were not giving me my employee file as I had requested in my initial email. Then it was my turn to speak.

The thing with me is that you can come at me like you are crazy and I would still be civil with you. In spite of her rotten attitude, I thanked her and began to patiently explain my side of the issue for the umpteenth time. I calmly pointed out that I only sent mails to the company executives because she had refused to reply my first email, and that I knew that the company would not hand me my employee file. I purposely asked in order to test their integrity, which turned out to be in short supply.

I would have to write a complete book on the details of this phone call alone, so I'll save you the trouble. In a nutshell, the Vice President and manager of the Human Resources department of the company that I had diligently and loyally served for fourteen years ambushed me. They accused me of being a bad manager, yet this was the first I was hearing of it in fourteen years! Might I add that I had physically seen the Human Resources manager only one time in my life, fourteen years ago. I had met the Vice President of HR just once as well, over ten years ago. These folks had never worked with me, never been out with me in the field, yet they wanted to criticize my work ethic.

This company's staff turnover was high! They had fired managers over integrity issues while I had constantly held my position with the highest level of responsibility and dignity, yet two people who were supposed to protect and help employees slandered me over the phone??? That was not all. The VP of HR then brought up the termination of another employee that I had given with my boss's approval. He accused me of firing this girl wrongfully, with the manager of Human resources as his hype man, yelling angrily in the background. They were by far the most unprofessional people I had ever dealt with. By the way, this employee whose employment I had supposedly terminated "wrongfully" was falsifying patient information, and I saw it with my very eyes. I had to ask them if they would have preferred that I simply looked the other way as a manager in a healthcare company.

They simply could not justify my "white" boss's unfair and unprofessional actions in skipping to the "final" stage of writing me up without so much as an offense. He had only just become my boss at the end of August the previous year and here he was already placing my head on a platter.

As the call was ending, the VP of Human Resources then mentioned that everything that was said on the call should remain between the three of us. "What???" I thought. Had they lost their minds? They had spent the duration of the phone call bombarding me with slanderous accusations and lies, and now, I was just supposed to keep my mouth shut on how they had treated me? No! They had the wrong guy. That was not a secret I was going to keep, because no one should ever have to go through the verbal and mental abuse I experienced at the hands of these two… and yes, they were both white.

It was in that moment that I decided I would NEVER again subject myself to such people or allow myself to be forced into a spot where anyone would speak to me as though they owned me. The problem with black people, I included, is that we become loyal to the wrong things. I was loyal and faithful to a system where I had to continually prove myself. I realized that I had been fighting to stay upright since I started with this company, and I felt that pressure because I was often the only black person in the organization for varying periods. We would get a black employee here and there but never long enough to stay. So, as I ran the team, I already walked on eggshells, and then this new boss, who didn't even get to know me, carelessly places me in an unfair category, forgetting that in spite of the company's high turnover, my tenure was over ten years standing strong.

They conveniently forgot how accurately their revenue was deposited every night and work was completed without incidence every day. Even when employees didn't show up, I kept the team going, and corporate never received a complaint from me until now; I was never an attention seeker or a troublemaker. But at this point, I was done with them.

The only way that black people can positively navigate society in America is to first accept that racism is still very much around in America, and prejudiced people are still living all around us. This black skin is still a target for injustice. This acceptance must then birth our change. We have to "become" the change agents that we seek. White people are never really going to admit to racism or the fact that blacks are treated unfairly… they are white!

We must, therefore, focus on ourselves and break the color barriers inadvertently imposed on our minds more than one hundred and fifty-three years ago. We now have the responsibility of correcting some things. I am not even going to focus on white people in this book as there is no point beating a dead horse. Rather, I'd like to focus on us as a black race, and how we can improve life for ourselves. We are already here; we are not going anywhere, and we are multiplying by the day so, no one can eradicate us.

I encourage us to then move from colorism issues to becoming effective parts of a cohesive race. For years, the colonizers knew that there were strength and unity in our numbers, hence, their ultimate job was to manipulate our emotions, pitting us against one another in such a way that we could never be united. To embrace who we truly are, we need to start teaching our children to understand their heritage. You can gather books and other literature for children around you to help them learn more about the pride of black culture.

For anyone to value themselves, they must know who they are and where they're from. When children understand how to be black and proud of it, they would never have to struggle with their self-esteem because of race. We have to cease to empower the concept of the white man by no longer focusing unnecessarily on such conversations in our homes. This will strengthen black pride in your home and produce a generation in whose minds have no limits.

For those that like to organize face-to-face interactions, we can create black esteem groups that can hang out in safe public spaces and discuss the advancement of black people, rather than what the "white man" has done. We already know what the white man is capable of. So, let's not waste any more time and effort feeding it, as what you keep speaking of will grow because your words feed it.

Let's focus on the next generation and think of how we can empower our own children from within? How can we raise the next generation to be fearless, and embolden black men and women? By continuing to learn about the great black ancestors of America, and actively presenting their heroic acts to the evolving minds of our children. This way, they would realize that white superman is only a fictitious character seen on television.

If we must create a new generation that reasons without limits, then we must re-create our own selves first. We must begin to consciously wash out thoughts and feelings of colorism. For instance, when you are watching television with your children, you cannot say things like "I'm sick and tired of seeing all these "light-skinned people." Children are products of their environment, and they imitate what they see. We must plant seeds of positivity and greatness in them both actively and passively, by raising them to think beyond the borders of black and white. And we must start now.

Own

Now is the time to start owning our race! Yes, we need to own our blackness and be unapologetic about it. Even though I am not focusing on white people in this book, allow me to present a potent example; white people are very loyal and trusting of one another. One can line up a drug-addicted white person next to a corporate working-class black person and white people would still defend their "own."

We are probably the only race that's skeptical and distrustful of one another, but we are all we have, and if other races cannot seem to trust us and we're also unable to trust one another, then our strength is called to question. You must remember that this division and distrust are just mechanisms and manipulative tactics that were planted in our minds in the past. A people with a sense of ownership and togetherness will certainly thrive and succeed, especially where the possibility of turning on one another does not exist.

I have traveled into rural America and seen white people living in worse conditions than the supposed poor blacks, yet one thing stands out about them; they hold on to the esteem and pride of their white ancestry. They own it! Most black folks who succeed in climbing their way to the top tend to become "bourgeois" and snobbish, not wanting to look back at the place they came from because some blacks link success to a certain behavior. No matter how rich or successful we are as black people in America, we are still going to experience some form of racism.

Black American parents have to own the responsibility of encouraging their children to do better and think bigger. The system is already set up in a seemingly unfavorable way, but if we start teaching our children that they can change things, they will grow up believing that. Whether or not that child will go to college, you will identify and help to groom their other gifts as well. In truth, we need more engineers, science majors and technology majors in the black community. We need people who are adequately educated to occupy positions that would significantly contribute to development. We need more lawyers who can successfully fight "the system" within the law. Regardless of all of these, the most important thing is to help our children identify their unique gifts and become the best of them. Ownership also means accountability followed by responsibility. I am not saying we are not a responsible people, but we need to take even more responsibility for what happens to us and how much progress we can make and be accountable to one another. Have you noticed how we jeer at our own? I have never seen on Twitter, Facebook or Instagram, a situation in which white people tear each other down… not even Asians.

In spite of the current presidents' shortcomings, the white people who don't necessarily like him still won't publicly humiliate him. They may only mildly call him out on his ways in order to keep him accountable. However, black people still aim to humiliate and tear one another down publicly. And these days, they would take screenshots of private messages and air them in public.

If we keep doing these degrading things to one another at home and in the public eye, we would only be creating an unhealthy "normal" for our children. We must set an example of good practices for them. They should not think it is okay to throw an empty paper bag out of a moving car. It bothers me whenever I travel through a predominately black run-down neighborhood, popularly called the hood, and notice how littered and unkempt the environment is. These are our neighborhoods, and we must be responsible for taking care of them. It is hard to change the narrative when we keep fitting right back into it.

I had a black employee who once told me quite proudly that she was looking through her phone frequently because she had to periodically check on her fifteen-year-old daughter for whom she had just bought a car. One would assume that was a great thing, except that she was actually keeping tabs on her daughter because she was driving without a permit. Hence, the young girl had to text her every time she made it to school and back home. Nope folks, her fifteen-year-old daughter had not taken a written driving course required to be on the right side of the law!

I assumed this employee felt comfortable giving me the extra information about her daughter because I am also black. If you teach your children that it is okay to break the law, then you cannot cry foul when "the system" comes after them for breaking laws. We must not encourage this type of behavior. My assumptions are that she felt comfortable with her daughter driving without a license because she herself had seen and done it before. Yet the truth is that if her baby-girl had gotten in a car accident and someone else was involved and injured, or worse, the law would go after the mother, as the driver was below the age of eighteen.

Then some of you would want to hold up signs saying, "free so and so." No, not if that person broke the law. It's really hard to address the very real issues of injustice and ill-treatment of black Americans when we continue to fall into a stereotype that breaks the law. You cannot cry "Injustice!" On the one hand, while breaking the law on the other; it doesn't work that way.

There was a brother, a rapper, who went to prison and most black people got their panties in a bunch over it. So, in my usual manner, I resisted the urge to react out of emotion but instead proceeded to dig into this man's past and found out that he was in violation of his probation. Of course, there are consequences for such offenses regardless of who you are and how much you're worth. In my opinion, he should have in fact made every effort to stay away from breaking the law, because of his celebrity status.

You cannot then expect people to hold up signs in protest. Dear black people, we've got to do better! Like we usually say at the dinner table, "The system is not for us, it's meant to go after us." Since we already know that, why don't we start teaching one another a new way of life and beat the system at its own game by giving it nothing on us? I know some may not agree that this will make much of a difference but imagine that we begin to have more blacks in living within the law, then we can build a solid case when we get pulled over unjustly.

But we have no case if our car tags are expired, and that's why we got pulled over in the first place, or if we are carrying dirty guns. Although I am aware that a black man who had a gun permit still got killed by the police, we cannot let such terrible experiences scare us from being on the right side of the "system." If another victim was gunned down by officers who found a legally owned gun on him, we can march for this and use it to our advantage. We can actually claim greater injustices if we are within the law. This is not to say that those that have been murdered by police officers were not in accordance with the law.

On the flip side, have you noticed that every time a black man is gunned down, the usual excuses are that "He was reaching for something…" or "He had a gun or drugs on him?" Who is there to defend these victims? We need to be responsible for each other. We need more people who would record these events as they happen in order to accurately tell the victim's side of the story. You do not have to be afraid of any consequences. We need more black civilian police and neighborhood watches.

The emphasis here is really to create a new generation, a new way of thinking and hopefully to salvage some of us who are stuck in the current way of thinking. Change is not going to automatically come because we have hoped for it; it will come when we put in the work. Our children have to know that we contribute to society by paying our fair share of taxes and living according to the "laws" of the land.

Mothers, if you feel stuck raising your child in a bad neighborhood, consider moving somewhere else. You have to want this for your children more than anything. I get that we get comfortable in certain neighborhoods where the majority look like us, but I also know that you can relocate if you are not satisfied with the prevailing social climate in your metropolitan area.

Years ago, I mentored a young mother, who had two children. She lived in the city and complained about gunshots and unrest in her community. She grew up in that city, so it had become her comfort zone. Two years later, after submitting her name to the Reduced Housing Program of the state I lived in at that time, she was granted a place in the county. This county was a choice area, with probably just a few black people, but it was a great neighborhood. Heck! Even I couldn't afford to live there at that time. But when she told me, I was excited for her and encouraged her to move, as it would be a great start. The school districts were phenomenal, and there would be no more gunshots every night; she could actually raise her children in a much better environment than she grew up in.

Guess what? She did not move. She allowed her fear of leaving all she had ever known, keep her in a drug and crime infested neighborhood. My heart sank, but she was a grown woman, so there was little I could have done. She was the one who was responsible for her children's environment and upbringing. I could not judge her for her decision because I was not in her shoes. I never grew up in a community like hers.

However, if we continue to refuse to change ourselves, our minds, and our way of life, then we lose our right to complain about the "white man." The white man isn't capable of taking everything away from us as a people. It's our mental enslavement concerning our value that keeps us bound in this vacuum of struggle, hustle, and handouts.

If the white man could hold an entire black race down, then we shouldn't have the likes of Aliko Dangote, Strive Masiyiwa, Mohammed Al-Amoudi, Mike Adenuga, Robert Smith, Michael Jordan, Michael Lee-Chin, Mohammed Ibrahim, <u>Oprah Winfrey</u>, <u>Isabel dos Santos</u>, <u>Folorunsho Alakija</u>, or <u>Patrice Motsepe</u>.

Nsehe Mfonobong wrote that out of the 2,043 people on the 2018 FORBES list of billionaires, eleven of them are black. (*Mfonobong Nsehe, March 7, 2018, Forbes. Com*)

The names I underlined above are those of women, and everyone on that list is a black billionaire. We have to begin to raise a new crop of confident, proud and empowered black boys and girls. Our table talks of what the white man can or can't do must cease. Now is the time to empower our children. We need more black male and female billionaires. We are not limited; the only thing that limits us is our minds and the way we perceive one another.

The richest man to have ever lived and have a net worth of close to a trillion dollars was an African man of royalty named

Mansa Musa, and as you read above, four out of the eight are Western Black Billionaires, while the rest are African Billionaires. I am not bragging, but only hoping that your mind opens up to the opportunities, and actual possibilities of investments that are readily available for you in Africa, especially when you feel that you don't want to place your US dollars in the white man's hands in America.

React

I am about to step on some toes, but for the greater good of my race, I will gladly do so! Why are we always quick to react to how we are treated by the other races? We often respond as though these ill-treatments were surprising to us. I don't like the injustice any more than you do, but we cannot also continue to beat a dead horse. The white people of America are not going to notice or address racism until they want to. Therefore, we cannot continue to whine at every turn of events. We must move forward while keeping an eye on the enemy.

A *sista* (black woman) made a video on how she felt that the entertainment industry should pay her a certain amount because she knew she deserved it, which was great. Then, she went on to ask black America to boycott the concerned organization's activities with her. I thought that was awkward; how do you ask me to cut off my subscription, so YOU can fill your pockets? Don't get me wrong, I am always supportive of black culture, at least the logical parts of it. If this woman had a track record of giving half of her proceeds to black communities, then I would've stood in solidarity, but the only community her proceeds would be going to was her family. I just had to pass.

I wonder if her strategy achieved anything, as I didn't turn my subscription off. I had to catch up on all my episodes of *How to Get away with Murder*. Did the boycotts work in the case of the little black boy who modeled in a monkey shirt for that popular clothing store? Note that this happened in January or February, around tax time. Who was going to boycott a clothing store in the black community at that time of the year?

Now let's talk about the many talented black actors, actresses, and artistes who have rightfully expressed their dissatisfaction with the treatment they have gotten from Hollywood and the awards over the years? I mean, I do feel their pain; they do all this work and are not being acknowledged. However, I'm not sure the planned boycotts of the awards really worked either.

Black Lives Matter—indeed! Black lives certainly matter, but our babies still keep getting shot.

I could go on and on. But I must say that I have the utmost respect and love for every person and organization that made efforts and facilitated resistance on behalf of Black people. I appreciate their courage, and I do not mean to discredit their attempts, but we really need to ask ourselves if these activities have gotten us the results we need.

As an African on the outside looking in, I believe that Black America is at a vantage point. I am not ignoring the harsh realities of unfair treatment, I am just saying that while we stage the protests, let's also begin to steer our children towards their passions, whether its law or business. White people have been fighting black people silently through the "system," often represented by the law. We need to raise a generation that is not only knowledgeable about protests but also about getting protective and profitable policies written into law. The possibilities are endless if we can just have more minorities within the law system or even on "the Capitol hill."

Though racism is very much alive, please understand that the white policy makers and influencers on the hill are not necessarily racist. Sometimes, it's just the fact that they don't have people like you and me within the system that can vote against an unfavorable Bill. I cannot expect the House of Representatives and the Senate, made up of a majority of rich, privileged white people to ever understand why certain resources and or benefits are beneficial for minority communities. They don't know the struggle and if they have never been through it, why defend the Bill? It does not impact on them in any way, so they are mostly uninterested.

But if we raise a generation that is passionate about Black people and are intentional about making real changes, then that same energy needs to be invested into law school. There is strength in numbers, so the fewer the minorities are in lawmaking, the fewer the chances you get to have your concerns adequately addressed.

Now is the time for us as black people to put our best foot forward and make it happen. No more feeding into the handicap of the "white man." We must learn to react by accomplishing more and plotting our own progress. Now, let's consider the same black lady who asked us to boycott a big entertainment company because in her words, "there was lack of diversity and she felt that she was discriminated against." I just think that with her amazing talent, she could've handled her own special and used the footage to bid other companies. She could have reaped handsomely, had she taken her show on the road in the U.S. or even to places like Africa or Europe. You all just don't understand how we love black culture in Africa. She could have gone from North Africa to South Africa or even toured Europe.

The exhausted and emotionally drained black actors and actresses of Hollywood are talented enough to start their own. How do you think Hollywood got started? Why do you think Jewish people became successful after they had been the oppressed?

We as black people are always quick to react out of emotion, and rightfully so too. If they are slaying our babies, our emotional pain must seep out somehow. However, after we are done complaining and cussing everyone out. What's next? When I called my father to discuss the upsetting conversation I had with the Human Resources Manager and Vice President of my organization, he shared a similar experience on his own job, years before I was born! I am talking about Africa in the 70's before our independence. Do you know how that cut deep into my soul?

Hearing my ultimate hero telling me about the discrimination of the "white man" and what he went through. I felt sick to my stomach. Look, folks, something needs to change. We cannot keep jumping from generation to generation, pointing fingers at the "white man." After completing my book,

Black, A misunderstood Race (*Navigating America in Black Skin*), I had an epiphany, which birthed this book. That epiphany demanded for an uncomfortable way of thinking among blacks and a drastic change among the black people.

I do understand that it's easier to write a book than to practically live out those same ideas but if we want a difference, we have to react differently. My sincere hope and desire is for all black people in the world to be empowered in our identity, and actually understand that we can accomplish anything despite the odds.

The universe sends us messages, and these messages only make sense if we pay attention. The entertainment and sports industry have been largely run by black people. I cannot pass up an opportunity to talk about the movie *Black Panther* which became the second highest Marvel opener of all time with a reported budget of $200 million. As of April 2018, the movie had reportedly risen to about $1.3 billion in sales. From 2009 till 2017, Barack Obama, a black man, was the people's president.

Sometimes, when I look at these two milestone events, just a few of the many events feats achieved by black America, I can't help but think that the universe is sending us a message. It is as though God is saying; "What other sign do you people need?" The universe seems to be asking us how long we are going to continue to be victims of a "system" that will never recognize us.

When they called a boycott in the movie industry because black actresses and actors are not getting enough work or winning awards for the talent they truly have, then why not create our own Hollywood? Look at the universal signs… we can do it with a determined cohesiveness. Together, we can. Hollywood was started by a Jewish community.

The Jewish community of America grew sick and tired of being castigated and discriminated against, that they started their own clothing stores, their own furniture stores and so forth. They created their version of almost everything, and today, the Jewish people are one of the wealthiest races in America.

The Jewish people of America didn't mope around with a victim's mentality, because Lord knows their past was not pleasant either. Rather, they accomplished all they did right in the face of active resentment and injustice from the white people. Today, most Jewish-American people have accumulated enough wealth for generations to come and are now hated even more by the white neo-Nazi-radical supremacists.

I keep wondering why Black Hollywood still feels the need to beg white people for opportunities. We have enough potential to rule the entertainment industry or successfully create our own. A dynamic black production is long overdue, and we can create our own awards that cause the existing ones to pale in comparison. We could literally pull this off bigger than we think but we have to be united. Europe and African markets will accept our work, whether its music, art, movies or other creative ideas. Why do we have to limit our scope to what America wants for the blacks? It's not like America has been paying us any heed since slavery. Their dismissive ways are repulsive, and that should drive black America to explore a world beyond them.

Every time we think we are protesting, America turns away from us. We take a knee, they say we have disrespected the flag; the very flag that should inspire justice and fairness. We march and boycott, and they quickly call our organized groups "hate groups," even though America really never condones hate groups or the Ku Klux Klan within its borders.

Black America, when are you going to open your eyes and see that America has never tried to really listen to us? If they did, they would understand the reasons for our protests and proffer solutions. Instead, like the days of enslavement, we are not considered human enough to be head. They deny our experiences, justify their hate and above all, dismiss our pain and suffering.

I am not saying we need to ignore a painful past. I'm only suggesting that we allow that painful past to propel us into the next paradigm of the new blacks… the Black Elitists. We need to rise up together as a collective body because we can actually attain great success by ourselves. Understand that no other race will stick up for blacks, but blacks themselves. So, we better get it together.

Now is the time to put our foot on the pedal and drive. We have signs like the Black Panther Movie and a Black president, so what's our deterrent really? Do you know that you do not even have to depend on white America's dollars? This is the time to get out of your comfort zone and make sacrifices. Certain African countries are looking for you. They've got land, and a chunk of business opportunities just waiting to be tapped into. The value of the U.S. dollar is high, and this is great for expansion. Black America needs to grow beyond America. If you've ever tuned into my podcast, you've already heard me dispel the lie of the colonizer.

From an African to you, we have nothing against you. I remember how it used to irk me when black people would ask me why Africans didn't like them when we first moved to America. I had no knowledge of such a thing, and my feelings would be hurt. I had such great admiration for the black American culture growing up, and here I was, finally in the U.S, and my kinsmen thought I didn't like them. What a complete misconception!

We need to learn to decipher what is true and what is not. Dear black people expand your thinking. Sometimes, success is locked in places you never imagined. It doesn't even have to be Africa, it can be Europe. I'm just saying, stop buying those high-end dollar shoes and instead, travel and invest in other places most white Americans won't go. There is nothing wrong with places like Jamaica and Cancun. And if you want to focus on investing and growing your money in America, that's good too, but don't complain about the "white man." Just remember that Mansa Musa was the richest man of all time and he was from Africa. The greatest thing about living in America is you can always present fresh ideas to other countries and still be ahead because of how fast things move in America.

Here's another example of the Agenda; the Million Women March of 2017. What a great collaborated effort that was, right? But if feminism were as all-encompassing as it appeared on that day in Washington, why don't we have that same number of women, estimated at 500,000-1,000,000, readily available to stand up for issues affecting black and brown women? **Immigration** and **Racial equality** were two issues that stood out for me of all the issues for which they were supposedly marching.

If this is true, how come I haven't seen this type of turn out when our black babies are being slain by cops? Sure, they are male, but they came out of a "feminine" part, right? What about all the times that the Immigration Customs Enforcement has torn families apart from East coast to West coast, arresting "mothers" or children at the borders and throwing them in jails? Isn't this an *"immigration"* issue? Sure, I am a woman, but you see, I am not a feminist. I know who I am and how to advocate when I need to.

I don't need an "umbrella" group that states what they believe on paper, but only march when the mood is right for "them" and when it suits their agenda, yet women are still getting paid less, black actresses are still being treated unfairly in Hollywood and in corporate America, and black mothers whose sons have been ripped out of their lives stand in the sidelines hopeless. But we have feminist groups, right? All I can say is, black women, don't be deceived, and be sure that your affiliates truly share your struggles. All of that being said, I am not against the feminist group and its participants. Nas said it best on the 5th track of his 2018 *Nasir album, "Inclusion is hellav-a-drug."*

Never

The only way we can progress as a group is to never forget the past but learn from it and start narrating the stories of our people to our children. This is called verbal history and is necessary because western education will not tell the complete truth about the history of the black person in America. They would rather sell the ridiculous idea that we simply sold one another. This often makes me wonder; who were the chiefs and what tribes were involved if indeed we sold one another?

We need to realize that we are the only race that doesn't have our own strong written history. The western books read in our schools have been interpreted by the descendants of the colonizers so, naturally, their version of history pushes the agenda that black people hated one another so much that they sold one another as slaves. They conveniently leave out the truth of how we despised the colonizers, and how we suddenly found out that they had begun to steal our land and kill our people with guns, just for their selfish interests.

Please believe me when I say there was a battle to keep our lands and preserve our people, and you will find these stories in books about the heroes of Africa, of whom some were actually women.

In my home country in Africa, the ancient stories say that we had a spirit medium, who warned us about the colonizers, she was in the forefront and encouraged my ancestors to fight until the literal "bloody-end." The King at that time found out that he had been deceived by the "catholic church" under the guise of missionary work. That was simply a strategy of the colonizers (whites and Portuguese) to penetrate the African tribes. After King Lobengula found out about the British asserting themselves over our land, the King took all the warriors and anyone else he could to go and fight the British army. My ancestors were outnumbered by their guns, and thousands of people died.

Legend has it that after killing our people, the British army found *Ambuya Nehanda and Sekuru Kaguvi,* the spirit mediums, and hung them. However, Ambuya Nehanda said these words in our language; "I am not dying. Instead, my blood will run and course deep in the earth, and my presence will be around until the land has been rightfully

returned to its people." (That literally gives me goosebumps every time I think of it).

I have more stories to tell but very few pages, however, the morale of the story is that as my grandmothers passed these stories to us, the generations to come will never forget how our land was stolen from us. This history is the same for black people living in America. Our intention isn't to pass on a victim mentality. Rather, it is to teach our children and generations to come about the pride of the black ancestors who fought very hard to resist the oppressor. Let your children know about all the Black American heroes and how they fit into your narrative today, for an empowered person is a very powerful person!

Freedom

The great philosopher Bob Marley once said in the lyrics of his song **Redemption Song;** "E*mancipate yourselves from mental slavery, none but ourselves can free our minds…"*

This is exactly what we as black people have to work on. I know that we are not computers and we cannot go into our minds and press *Ctrl+Alt+Delete* and suddenly begin to think differently. But the fact that in 2018, we can agree on one thing, life *isn't fair for the black folk in America"* means our perception is still accurate and our minds are sharp. We must now move forward. We can no longer focus our energy on the oppressor because it would only keep us mentally oppressed, and that is why I appeal to you all, to change your focus.

We already know the problems, but how are you going to improve the coming generation? How are you going to encourage your daughter to be the next Billionaire or Trillionaire? How are we as a race going to come together and harness our power? The Jewish community chose to progress by moving forward together and unshackling themselves from mental slavery, in spite of the tragedies they had suffered.

If slavery was allegedly abolished in 1865, then how do we free our minds right now in 2018, and start seeing life through renewed eyes and not in *Massa's* (Master of the plantation) eyes? Some of us have those tendencies of *Massa* because they were subconsciously imparted into our psyche by our relatives. I am pretty sure our kin didn't understand the power of such words in keeping a people mentally enslaved.

Massa's eyes represent a view that pits black people against other black people based on complexion. It seeks to assert that one dark complexion is better than the other even though in reality, we are all black. Massa's eyes see material possession as a success, when such people may not even be able to pay rent. It is a concept that divides black people along the lines of class and teaches some black people to hate their own complexion. Massa's eyes are those of betrayal to blacks and loyalty to the oppressor, at the expense of their own people.

#TheAgenda   Mansa Mnēmē

I think that if my parents grew up telling me all the things the "white man" did and all the things the "white man" wouldn't allow us to do, then I might have been mentally trapped. Why would I even want to try to become anything great, when it seemed that the white man would always hinder my progress regardless of whatever I tried to achieve? Yet, in actual fact, he might not even be the root cause of my current problems.

I am pushing for the black community to impart words of wisdom into the minds of our children. I am calling for a new way of thinking, as it all begins in the mind. I, for example, never lost my African pride even when I moved to America. I was, and still am a confident and proud black person. That is why most of my initial conversations with black Americans were, "What do you mean they won't let us?" I could never understand that obstacle, no matter how much black Americans tried to explain it to me about the "white man." I simply refused to believe that another human being could limit me.

I have mentioned on my blog, podcasts, and YouTube videos that it wasn't until I moved to the Midwest of America that I discovered I was black, but even then, the mental notion of another person holding me down was and is still not present.

Please understand that I am not dismissing the statistics, or the concept of white privilege, and the fact that a black student has to have more degrees than his white counterparts. However, it's a win-win for our people, for the more educated we are, the better for us. We must not allow the happenings around us to snuff out our hope.

The oppressor feeds himself off power and dominance, and if we cower to his every whim, he gains more power. We can start businesses. You do not have to work for the "white man" if you do not want to. I am discovering that one can do a lot in America, without the white man's permission. There are so many opportunities for a sole proprietorship. We have big and diverse organizations such as Google and Amazon opening up some of their businesses so that people like you and I can become independent.

Freedom from racism starts in our minds. We have to avoid things, actions and words that keep us oppressed. Imagine a world where all the white people in America were no longer racists yet in our minds as black people, we still view the white skin as oppression…of what benefit would that be to us? This is why we have to do the mental work first because as long as the black person's mind is still enslaved, he will never be free.

Rumors

As we all know by now, knowledge is the foundation of all wisdom. We are no longer on some primitive "plantation" in the distant past, and we can no longer rely on "he-said, she-said." We are still guilty to react to issues based on hearsay without taking the time to investigate further in order to fully decipher the information. In this chapter, which is a piggyback of the *Freedom* chapter, I'd be addressing a few things that possibly drag us down as a people.

I found out about the enslavement of black Americans when I moved to America, at the age of sixteen. That type of information is traumatizing at that age. I didn't know how to digest it, and what bothered me the most was the fact that we were never taught this information in our schools in Africa. We were taught about World War 1 and World War 2, and we had to memorize Woodrow Wilson's fourteen points, only for me to find out later that he didn't care much for black people. I said all that to say that countries in Africa were physically free of the colonizer although he had already left behind his seeds of manipulation through the education system. I feel strongly the slavery history of our people was left out of our education system because such knowledge would have infuriated blacks everywhere. It was just easier for the oppressor to tamper with the truth of how black people got dispersed across several locations against their own will. Yet we Africans live in our countries and learn the faulty white man's history. My thoughts led me to do some more research on black history, and this helped me to unravel the pattern of the oppressor.

A defeated person is one that is defeated in the mind, so as long as they keep teaching the white man's history to Africans, we would never know the truth about other black people. And as long as the curriculum in American schools is focused on western history, then the black person in America won't know the truth about his heritage.

This is why I suspect that the rumor in America about Africans not liking black Americans was clearly set up by the oppressor to continually keep the black race divided. Take note of these tactics. The only way you will ever discover the truth is to dig deep into the history of your people and read books by African American authors. Now is the time to reconnect with who you are as a person and who your children are.

However, if you also decide that you do not care much for finding out anything about your African or Native American heritage, I do not judge you for it.

Understanding our history helps us avoid the pitfalls of tomorrow. Understanding the course of history and questioning some of the details presented by western authors also brings forth the truth. I remember researching information about the spirit medium that encouraged our people to fight the British army back in the 1800's and finding that almost 99% of the information was written by western authors because it clearly painted my people as the bad guys and the colonizer as the hero. To think that such an army actually slaughtered my people, hung the spirit medium and then stole our land. If any of the colonizers were to admit in 2018 that they had indeed stolen these African nations without permission, then that action could've possibly placed the white citizens that occupied the stolen African land in harm's way because surely a revolt would happen.

Sometimes you don't even have to dig too deep into the original stories. You can just take a critical look at recent history. At the beginning of this book, I gave a summary of some of the happenings within a brief timeline in history, and I'm sure that between 1917 and 2016, there were more events. Studying and understanding what happened in Tulsa, Oklahoma teaches us a lot. For instance, I learned that it is possible for black people to come together and spend their dollars in a black community. I also learned that once a black community in America comes together in such a powerful way, they also have to stand guard and not get too comfortable. One should certainly enjoy the fruits of ones' labor but at the same time, watch carefully for your safety so that history doesn't repeat itself like in the Atlanta Race Riot of 1906, East St. Louis Massacre of 1917, the Chicago Race Riots of 1919, Greenwood, Tulsa, Oklahoma 1921, and the Rosewood Massacre in 1923.

Always remember that the oppressor uses manipulative tactics in the form of deceptive words intended to divide a group of people and stop them from ever forming a strong alliance.

Embrace

What is America doing to end racism? A whole bunch of nothing. Black America needs to understand by now, that if America didn't listen to Dr. Martin Luther King and the likes of Malcolm X and Marcus Garvey, they are even less likely to listen to us. The only way to prevail is to come together to embrace and help one another.

Right now, we are wasting time-fighting, betraying and making fun of one another. If you launch a Google search for assassinated *White supremacist* leaders, the only result likely to come up is that of a man who was part of the Klan, eventually murdered by his family in Missouri. Other than that, those searches would be a dead end. However, if you try launching a Google search for assassinated *Black leaders,* a good number of stories pop up. Why do you think that is? Well, most of these black leaders were probably sabotaged by their own people.

Even though black America felt a certain way about our brother Kanye, I figured he had a point (except the slavery being a "choice" statement), other than that his choice of words may have been wrong. And even if he meant it exactly as he said it, we mustn't throw it all away. Could it be that black America could have been further ahead and in social standing and wealth in comparison to "white America?"

Dr. Martin Luther King was assassinated, and though there is no evidence suggesting who tipped off the shooter, could it have been one of us? That is food for thought. Meanwhile, here are some facts; Marcus Garvey "tried" to help black America but was met with resistance from some rich black Americans. At the time that his ship was supposed to be making headlines as a big accomplishment, there were some black informants including his own captain that sabotaged the ship. Malcolm X was murdered by black people. Fred Hampton was killed by the Chicago police department, based on information provided by his right-hand man… a black man.

Does this narrative sound familiar? For Christians; *Genesis 25:29-34,* is a scripture about a brother who sells his birthright for lentil soup. His brother Jacob even questioned his sentiment, but Esau felt that he was about *to die* anyway so why even care? Please read this story and dig deeper till you get to the part where the brothers had to appear before their father. Life is punctuated by spoiler alerts, and nothing new happens under the sun. All the blessings that were supposed to be bestowed upon Esau went to Jacob, all because Esau didn't value himself.

I started off with a question: Is it possible that black America shouldn't be this far behind in wealth and relevance? Is it also possible that our ancestors in America sabotaged some of that growth as we still do today? Where would black America be if Dr. Martin Luther King got to finish his work? Or Malcolm X? Or Fred Hampton?

These men were the voices of the people; the voices of liberation. They were the people that chose to stand up against the odds and fight for us as a black people and yet, we betrayed them. Maybe if we admitted to this, our healing could finally begin. The black people who killed our leaders sold their birthrights for Lentil, a gross tasting soup. I'm highlighting its taste so that the analogy is clear. Esau could have sold his birthright for a filet mignon, fresh out of the backyard, since he was a hunter. But no, he sold it for some good-ol'-plain-Jane-soup.

David Duke, the former Grand Wizard of the Ku Klux Klan is still alive and thriving. And well engaged in his supremacist movement. No one killed him off, and none of his Klan members conspired to kill him. From all the research I've done on blacks and whites, the black leaders who were representing a good and possible change for black America were betrayed and killed by black people, while the man that spreads hate (*David Duke*), is alive and kicking in 2018.

How does this work, black America? I don't want to hear your conspiracy theories about the F.B.I or C.I.A on our leaders, because had we built a strong alliance, no one would have gotten to our leaders. How does anyone even accept to be an informant against their own people? We must indeed work on this tendency of being disloyal, and we must do it together.

I do not seek to castigate my own people, neither am I trying to assert that we would have been better off, had the black leaders been alive. I honestly don't know, because we never gave them a chance. What I do know is that some kind of change would have had to occur.

I followed the story of a black Pan-Africanist brother from America for some years. He started his passionate movement and had a brilliant and much-needed idea in place; he was going to introduce schools for black children. But because a few misinformed black Americans could not imagine why a black school would be necessary, they persecuted him! They went as

far as questioning his credentials, which resulted in having to go before a judge to defend his education. Once again, black America had betrayed yet another brother who was trying to look out for black children. Black schools are absolutely important if we must break the cycle of reading the white man's faulty history books.

This black Psychologist with a doctorate was aiming to do a good thing, yet it was wrongly perceived as a desperate effort to perhaps, enrich himself. The irony of it was that such opposing black bigwigs would donate to big non-profit organizations that would fund research with only a very small percentage of the proceeds. Whatever huge chunks were left ended up in the CEO's pockets, whose children are most likely in private schools or Ivy league colleges. This man was going to introduce a much-needed structure into the black community, black schools that would engender our pride and heritage. We must always remember that no one is going to save black people, but a black person.

If we're going to make progress as a people, we might as well start working together and mobilizing as a unit. This means we don't sell one another out for false freedom promised by the oppressor. When you are a stool pigeon, you are saying, "If the law reduces these events, then I will sell my own people." The law will NEVER protect you or other black people. Black people will protect themselves once unified. Once we start building bridges to help one another, we would be able to create our own "Black Wall Street." I have seen the power, strength, and determination of the black race so I am absolutely certain that it can be done. I insist that the only person that will care for a black person is another black person.

Every time I experienced overt racism, it happened in spaces where there was nothing but a white audience, and it was not like any of them attempted to comfort me. They simply looked my way and went right back to whatever they were doing, acting like nothing happened! Not all of white America is racist, I agree. But the tiny percentage that's not racist would rather wash their hands clean and act like they didn't see anything at all. What do you think happened in Oklahoma? It wasn't all the white people of the town that participated in the killings, but those who didn't participate hid and acted like they could not hear the screams or the smell of the burnt Negro bodies in the streets! We have to save ourselves, black people. White people will stick together, no matter what and how they feel about one another.

I was in corporate leadership for fourteen years, and my team comprised mainly of white women. These white women would individually throw one other under the bus when they were with me (individually), but when stuff went south, and I got yelled at by a white employee, none of these ladies said a word in my defense. They just gawked and acted like they didn't notice. I had learned to maintain my cool in the face of such outbursts because I wasn't going to lend credence to that *angry black girl* stereotype.

So, who's really got our backs?

I discussed this at length in an earlier podcast episode called *Our Community talk show*. I stressed that if black people must reach across the aisle, then we have to learn to take the high road and embrace everyone. In my book; *Black a Misunderstood Race,* I mentioned that we do not have to take "ownership" of black "appropriateness," If Kim K wants to rock cornrows, let her! If Bruno Mars is dope like a black artist, so be it! Who really cares who is using or emulating "black culture?" I actually think we should feel honored that other races embrace black culture the way they do. When I was in Africa, I emulated the black American culture, because it's that dope! Black American culture is a fad that is found all across the globe, from Asia to Africa. You walk into the clubs, and they are going hard on the dance floor with some rap or hip-hop music; that is a global influence.

I don't know too many other cultures that are emulated across the globe. Years ago, when I was back home in Africa, you were considered cool if you wore *Karl Kani* or *FUBU*. We need to stop expressing petty opinions about non-black people that emulate the black American culture. We need to stop criticizing the Afro-Latinas or Afro-Latinos. We cannot be the change agents we need to be if we are keeping tabs on what other races are doing. Who died and made us the only Ambassadors for the black culture?

I wish black America would even go that hard on social media to support their own. Let's re-direct our focus and energy, as there is a generation that needs to be steered in the direction of fresh possibilities.

Sticking together and helping one another builds empowerment, pride, and dignity… and an empowered people can't be limited. *Can't-nobody-tell-them-they-can't-do-anything!* We have to teach America how to treat us as a race, by showing them how we treat one another. We need to help our youth. There is no such thing as black-on-black crime…

crime is crime! Period. America is usually quick to introduce the black color when they want to cause division. If there is no such thing as white on white crime when white people kill one another, or Asian on Asian crime, then there should be no need to tag crimes involving black Americans by color. After all, other races are also committing several crimes every day, but we are not going to compare "apples to oranges." I mentioned the above example in order to highlight the racist agenda of America, not to make light of the death of our young men.

We have no time to slumber!

Evolve

I really enjoyed writing this book. I love my skin, I love my culture, I love my people, and I love my heritage! Like most people, I believe that we will get to the mountaintop together. I hope you had some aha-moments reading this book, and please understand it is not designed to mock, degrade or make light of the current realities of black people living in America. One thing I noticed when I was doing my research on the time period between 1917 and 2018 after the elections, is that the narrative for white supremacy is the same. The white elitist is still spilling hate and malice among his people to keep them divided because they know that a divided people are easy to dominate and conquer.

In 1917-1921, the middle and lower class white men who participated in the massacre in Oklahoma "Black Wall Street," did it essentially for their own pride. The fact remains that black America had done nothing wrong other than the fact that they were thriving and doing better than the white middle- and lower-class families. They simply could not let *niggers* get ahead. The

same feelings of jealousy and hate—fueled the other race riots of those times.

The real plot twist here is that the white middle and lower-class man is in the same boat with black America, but his hate tricks him into believing that he is superior… that and backing of lies from the white upper class who really don't care for anyone but themselves. Take our forty-fifth president, for instance, his moves appear to have been structured to establish his family and generations to come with our tax paying dollars.

However, we as a people need to start evolving. I urge black America to have some kind of global experience. Visit other climes. Most of the current billionaires I mentioned above are Africans who live in Africa. If only we realized how globally relevant black music and movies are today. Dear black Americans, there are several countries you can begin to explore, who would warmly embrace your skin, your heritage and more importantly, your black dollars.

Rise up, Black America! Now is your time!

#TheAgenda   Mansa Mnēmē

www.ingramcontent.com/pod-product-compliance
Lightning Source LLC
Chambersburg PA
CBHW031418040426
42444CB00005B/633